Ancient
Rome

Archaeology Unlocks the Secrets of Rome's Past

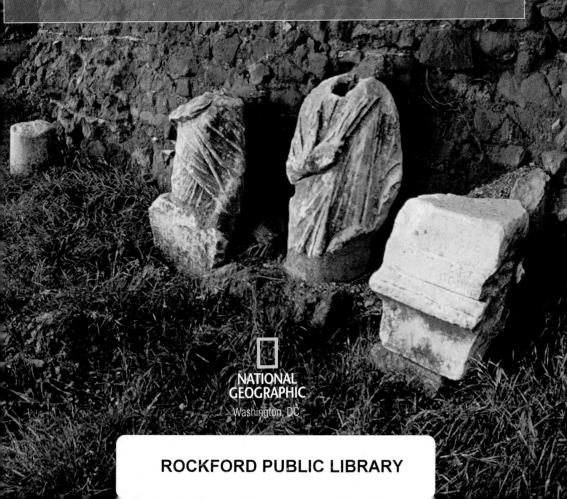

Ancient Rome

Archaeology Unlocks the Secrets of Rome's Past

By Zilah Deckker

Robert Lindley Vann, Consultant

NATIONAL
GEOGRAPHIC
Washington, DC

Contents

1

2

3

4

< In the band of relief carvings that spiral around Trajan's Column in Rome, some 2,500 figures tell the story of one of the Emperor Trajan's military campaigns.

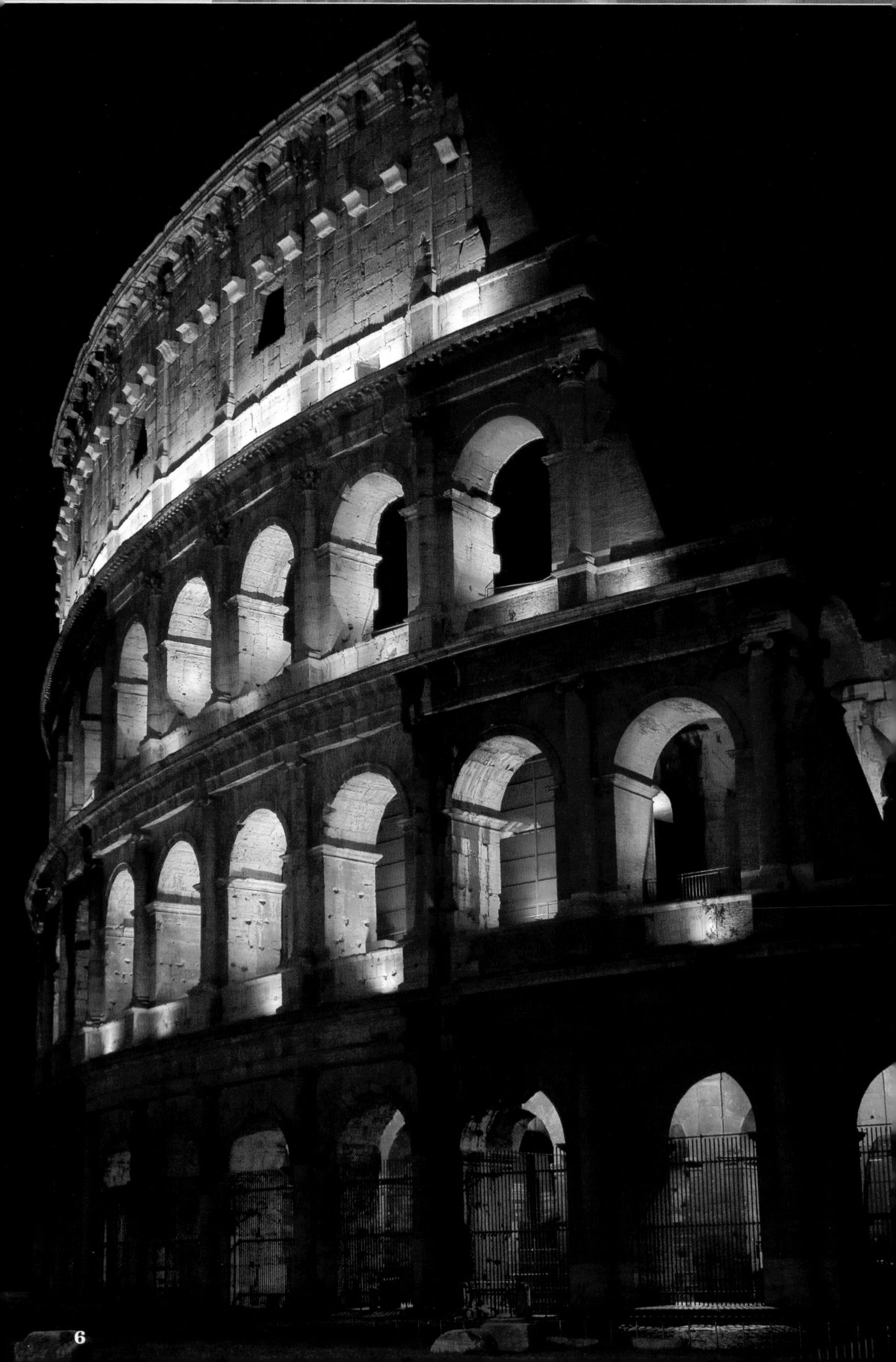

< The Colosseum in Rome is one of the most famous symbols of the Roman empire.
The arena was used as a venue for public events for over four centuries.

Map of the Roman Empire

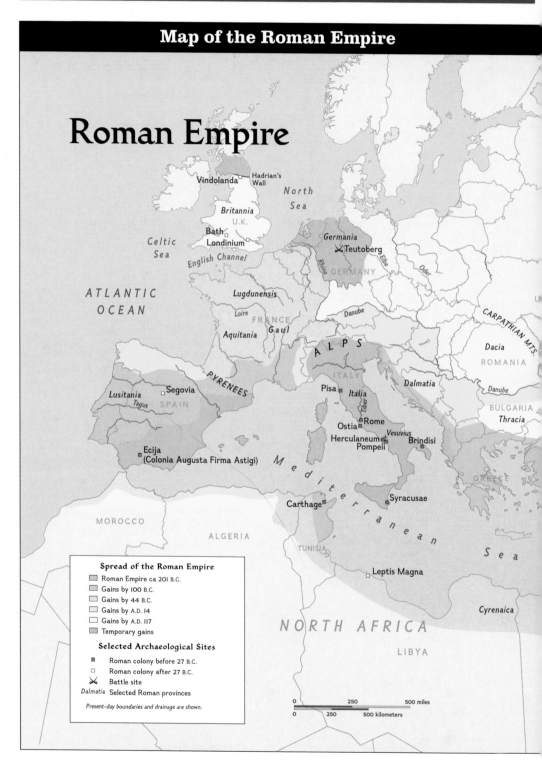

Roman Empire

Spread of the Roman Empire
- Roman Empire ca 201 B.C.
- Gains by 100 B.C.
- Gains by 44 B.C.
- Gains by A.D. 14
- Gains by A.D. 117
- Temporary gains

Selected Archaeological Sites
- ■ Roman colony before 27 B.C.
- ▫ Roman colony after 27 B.C.
- ✕ Battle site
- *Dalmatia* Selected Roman provinces

Present-day boundaries and drainage are shown.

| 0 | 250 | 500 miles |

| 0 | 250 | 500 kilometers |

A friend once told me that the more he studied the ancient Romans, the more he discovered just how much our civilizations have in common. This is probably true of any branch of history. People have not changed that much over the years. But our familiarity with ancient Rome is even stronger than that with most peoples of the past. We see their faces looking back to us from wall paintings and pieces of sculpture, we read their election notices painted on walls along their streets, and we can visit their homes, their temples, and their theaters. We read their books and live today under a system of law that has its origins in laws of their own times.

For the past six years I have been working in Pompeii, where one comes closest to re-living the lives of ancient Romans. Walking down street after street, block after block, one passes through neighborhoods of both modest and expensive homes, shops and warehouses, and the ever-present fast-food joints strategically located at the intersections of the busiest streets. As you will learn in this book, places like Rome, Caesarea, and Pompeii are magical for their ability to transport us to the past and make it come alive.

Robert Lindley Vann,
Maryland, 2007

Ancient Rome

The Growth of Rome

ca 800—200 B.C.

Beginning in about the tenth century B.C. farming peoples named Latins and Sabines settled on the later site of Rome. As a town emerged it fell under the rule of the neighboring Etruscans. The Romans rebelled and took power over their own city. In 509 B.C. they declared a republic. Through conquest and alliances the Romans gradually took power over the whole of the Italian peninsula, before also conquering parts of Iberia (in present-day Spain). This map shows Roman territory in 201 B.C.

The Late Republic

ca 200—27 B.C.

Rome's territory grew through a series of wars that lasted 300 years (Roman territory in 44 B.C., right). The Romans defeated Carthage, in North Africa; Greece; Syria in the Middle East; and France. They controlled the whole Mediterranean, which they called "Mare nostrum"— "Our sea." After nearly 500 years of republican government, a series of military leaders took power in Rome as dictators. The most famous was Julius Caesar. In 27 B.C. one of Caesar's descendants ended the republic when he declared himself "Imperator," or "emperor," with the title "Augustus."

< The Romans used glass to make vases and bowls and, beginning in the first century, for windowpanes.

Timeline of Italian History

800 B.C.	400 B.C.	0	A.D. 400
753 B.C. According to legend, founding of Rome by Romulus and Remus	**509 B.C.** Founding of the Roman Republic	**27 B.C.** Augustus founds Roman Empire	
		A.D. 79 Eruption of Vesuvius buries Pompeii and Herculaneum	**A.D. 117** Empire reaches its greatest extent
			A.D. 395 Empire divided into east and west

Farming peoples　　　Roman Republic　　　Roman Empire

< This carved clasp from the early first century A.D. probably held together parts of a soldier's uniform.

The Roman Empire

27 B.C.—A.D. 476

Under the emperors Roman territory reached its greatest extent in A.D. 117 (right). Such a huge empire was hard to hold together, and its borders came under attack from peoples whom the Romans named "Barbarians." In the fourth century Constantine made Christianity the religion of the empire. He created a new capital at Constantinople (modern-day Istanbul, Turkey). The empire was split in 395 into western and eastern sections. The western empire fell to the Visigoths in 476. As the Byzantine Empire, the eastern section survived until 1453, when it fell to the Ottoman Turks.

> This silver bowl was found in Arras, France, which the Romans ruled beginning in the first century B.C.

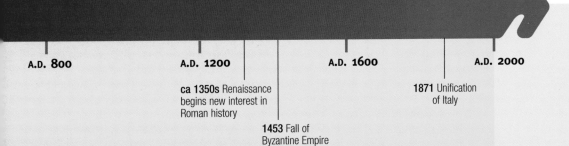

A.D. 800

A.D. 1200

ca 1350s Renaissance begins new interest in Roman history

1453 Fall of Byzantine Empire

A.D. 1600

1871 Unification of Italy

A.D. 2000

Yesterday Comes Alive

CHAPTER 1

How do we learn what we know about the past?

Every year the city council in Rome grants about 13,000 building permits. In most cities that would be routine. But in Rome, all building work has to be assessed by experts named archaeologists. Even graduate archaeology students help out on construction sites by recording anything that might be revealed when a hole is dug or a building knocked down. There is lots of work. For over 2,500 years the city has stood in a bend of the Tiber River in central Italy. Each time the river flooded, the Romans built their city higher, using older buildings as foundations for new ones.

< An archaeologist is lowered into a newly discovered vault beneath the streets of Rome in 2006. Every journey underground in the city is an adventure that might yield new surprises.

Beneath today's city are layers of old remains. If you dig down anywhere, you will hit a reminder of the ancient Romans.

Solid signs

Not all clues about the Romans are buried away. Some stand in the heart of the city, like the Colosseum where gladiators used to fight. Nor do all clues come from Rome, or even from Italy. Hadrian's Wall stands in northern Britain. The 73-mile-long (117-km) barrier was built to guard the edge of the Roman Empire. In North Africa, at the southern edge of the empire, cities have well preserved

V Built in about A.D. 50 the Roman aqueduct at Segovia in Spain carried water 9 miles (15 km) to the city. It was used late into the 20th century.

amphitheaters and theaters. In Segovia in north central Spain, water was until recently brought to the city by a Roman aqueduct.

The Romans left more traces over a wider area than almost any other ancient people. Homes, forts, ports, ancient shipwrecks, pottery, and weapons—even place names—are signs of the empire the Romans created beginning in about 400 B.C. At its height in A.D. 117 Rome's empire included all the lands around the Mediterranean Sea and most of Europe. The Romans ruled about 50 million people in what are now around 40 modern countries.

Roaming Romans

All over the empire are signs of Roman

power. Coins called *denarii* (singular, *denarius*) turn up everywhere. They were used by the traders who made the empire rich. They paid taxes to the government in Rome, which used them to pay for the empire. The Romans needed a strong army to conquer territory, as well as officials to organize it. From northern Europe to the Middle East straight roads still cut across the landscape. They were built by the Romans to make it easy to move both goods and troops. The roads were so well built that some are still in use. Other signs of the Romans are carved inscriptions all over Europe in Latin, the language of Rome. People throughout the empire could use Latin to communicate with one another.

Ruling such a large area was difficult. Eventually the empire grew weak and was overrun; Rome fell in A.D. 476. The cities were deserted; buildings fell into ruin. Outside of Italy, the civilization was largely forgotten for centuries—but it never completely disappeared.

Ancient language

Latin is one of the keys to learning about Rome. The Romans left many accounts and business records, as well as poems and plays, and histories of the empire. Many survived in libraries in the Byzantine Empire that replaced Rome in the eastern Mediterranean or in Islamic Spain.

Latin works are easy for experts to translate. That is unusual for ancient writing. The hieroglyphs of Egypt and the cuneiform of ancient Mesopotamia, for example, took scholars decades to decipher. But until the late 20th century most educated people in Europe and America could read Latin. They learned it at school, and studied ancient Roman works. Latin was also the language of the Roman Catholic Church, and was used in worship.

History's detectives

Another source of information about the Romans is physical remains, such as artifacts. These clues are often easy to find, but they may be hard to understand. That is the job of history's greatest detectives: archaeologists.

These experts carefully study all traces of an ancient civilization to put togethe a picture of how people lived. Some of their finds are spectacular, such as a grave full of gold objects. Most of the time, however, they find much smaller clues that they have to build into a larger picture. Sometimes the clues confirm details from other sources. At other times, they reveal something new

A hill full of holes

In 2006, archaeologists were working o the Palatine Hill, an ancient center of Rome. So many wealthy Romans built large villas that eventually all such homes became known as palaces, after the Palatine. About 500 buildings once stood on the hill but most are now buried. Those left on the surface are slowly crumbling. Making the building stable is the job of conservationists, wh specialize in preserving old buildings or artifacts. Their work is vital: Without them, ancient treasures might soon decay.

The archaeologists were working a the palace of Augustus, who became Rome's first emperor in 27 B.C. By the Rome already controlled a large area o territory around the Mediterranean Sea. Augustus built a luxurious palace for himself on top of the hill and one fc his wife, Livia.

< This stele, or carved slab, stood near a Roman road in Jordan. Latin Inscriptions have no punctuation and use many abbreviations, so they can be difficult to read, but they are a key source c information about the Romans.

> This sculpture of the wolf feeding Romulus and Remus is a symbol of Rome. The wolf was made in the fifth century B.C., but the figures were added nearly a thousand years later.

The archaeologists were trying to find out how stable the ruins were. They drilled small holes deep into the ground near the palace walls to take samples of earth and rock, a process known as coring. As they were drilling one hole, however, the drill suddenly broke through into empty space.

That was no surprise. The whole Palatine Hill is honeycombed with old rooms and tunnels. But it soon became clear that this was no ordinary discovery. When the team lowered a camera attached to a probe, they discovered a chamber 50 feet (15 m) deep. The walls glittered with what seemed to be mosaics and seashells.

Discovering a myth

Even in a city where the past is everywhere, it was a thrilling find. According to legend, Rome was founded by Romulus and Remus, twin sons of Mars, the god of war. The twins were abandoned in their cradle on the

Misleading myths?

The story of Romulus and Remus appears in the *Aeneid*, a long poem written by the Roman Virgil between 29 and 19 B.C. Virgil believed that Romulus and Remus were descendants of Aeneas, a Trojan prince. Aeneas was said to have fled to Italy after the city of Troy had been defeated by the Greeks in 1184 B.C. The story of Aeneas appears in the *Iliad*, a poem said to have been created by the Greek poet Homer in the eighth or seventh century B.C. Virgil wrote his poem soon after the first emperor came to power in Rome. He probably wanted to link Rome's greatness with that of the ancient city, as a sign that Rome was favored by the gods.

So far, there is no archaeological evidence to confirm the story of Romulus and Remus. However, in modern-day Turkey experts believe they have identified the ruins of Troy—and that the city was indeed defeated in the Bronze Age. Perhaps more old stories of Rome's past may turn out to hold at least a grain of truth.

Tiber River, where they were found by a wolf. She looked after them until they were discovered by a shepherd who brought them up. The site said to be the wolf's cave was sacred to the Romans. They made it a shrine on the Palatine Hill.

The experts in Rome believe that they have found the shrine, called the Lupercale (*lupus* is the Latin word for wolf). They argue it shows that the myth of the founding of Rome must be very old. The older it is, the more likely it is to reflect parts of the real story. Perhaps Rome really did have a

leader or leaders who founded a settlement on the Palatine Hill.

Other experts disagree: They say that the chamber may be a tomb. No one knows for sure. Archaeologists still have not found the entrance to the chamber. Until they do, they will not be able to study it more closely. For now, the mystery remains unsolved.

Myth and reality

In the legend, Romulus later killed Remus in a struggle about who was the leader of the new city. According to the Romans, Romulus became king on April 21, 753 B.C., and named the city after himself. The Roman calendar used dates based on the year 753 B.C., in the same way that Christians date their calendar from the birth of Christ.

▼ Archaeologists excavate an ancient fountain in the shadow of one of Rome's most famous monuments, the Colosseum.

In Chapter 2 you will see how new discoveries are pushing the date of the founding of Rome 300 years earlier than the myth claims. The whole city is a living museum. Even ancient drains help show how Rome grew. After the Romans set up a republic in the late sixth century B.C., they began to conquer new territory. Buildings became larger and more luxurious as the capital grew more wealthy.

In Chapters 3 and 4, you'll learn what life was like in the Roman Empire. From the deserts of the Middle East to the moors of northern Europe, remarkable finds introduce us to some of Rome's subjects. Chapter 5 explores two of the most famous of all ancient sites—the buried cities of Pompeii and Herculaneum. A volcanic eruption in A.D. 79 sealed the cities as time capsules for over 1500 years.

The Roman Empire fell in A.D. 476. As Chapter 6 shows, however, its legacy continued. Latin became the basis of languages such as Italian. Written works were preserved in the Byzantine Empire, the eastern part of the Roman Empire. Many old buildings survived, often because they were too big to be destroyed. When Europeans began to take a new interest in ancient Rome in the late Middle Ages, the clues were still all around them—and they still are today.

V The empire builders: Roman priests and magistrates take part in a parade to dedicate a new altar to Augustus after he became emperor.

The Heart of the Empire

CHAPTER 2

Why is Rome called the Eternal City?

In 2003 Darius Arya of the American Institute for Roman Culture directed students who were excavating in the Roman Forum. The dig was at the site of the house of Caligula, emperor from A.D. 37 to A.D. 41. Roman writers had said that Caligula was crazy. He made his horse Incitatus a priest and built it a house with a marble stable. The emperor appeared in the temple dressed as a god so that he could be worshiped. The stories were so

< Darius Arya sweeps away debris during the excavations of Caligula's home in the Forum. Some of Caligula's subjects accused him of being crazy.

ROMAN EMPIRE
ca 27 B.C. – 476 A.D.

| 200 | B.C. 0 A.D. | 200 | 400 | 600 |

unlikely that modern historians thought that they must have been exaggerated by the emperor's enemies.

Arya's team traced the walls of Caligula's home. They showed that the palace had been enlarged to join a Roman temple on the other side of the street. This was exactly what the Roman writer Suetonius had described about 70 years after Caligula died. Suetonius claimed that the emperor had used the temple as an entrance to his palace.

Such an act was a shocking sign of the emperor's pride. Arya said, "We have the proof that the guy really was nuts." Perhaps Caligula truly had begun to think that he was a god. And

perhaps that was one of the reasons why Roman troops assassinated him in A.D. 41.

Rome under the emperors

Caligula was one of the most eccentric emperors to rule Rome after Augustus. Many others were said to do crazy things, or to have been lazy or cruel. Others were talented and hard working. They worked to maintain and increase Rome's power and to make the city wealthy. Augustus himself claimed that he had found Rome a city of brick and left it one of marble.

Physical remains show that Rome was a busy jumble of narrow streets and small buildings where people often lost their way. The well-off lived in luxurious houses called *domus*. The poor lived in *insulae*, crowded

▽ The sun rises over the Roman Forum in this photograph taken from the Capitoline Hill, one of the seven famous hills on which the city stood.

multistory apartment houses. Public buildings—theaters, sports arenas, public libraries, bathhouses—were mixed in among the homes.

Waterworks

The heart of Rome was the Forum Romanum. This open space was originally a marketplace that grew up between the Roman Hills, on a low-lying marshy area that needed to be drained. The first public engineering work in Rome was the Cloaca Maxima, a large drain built using Etruscan techniques.

Water was vital: It had to be drained from some places but supplied to others for drinking and bathing. Engineers built a network of pipes and drains. Today, some of the best information about the growth of Rome still comes from underground. A group of speleologists—cave experts—formed Roma Sotterana (Underground Rome) to explore the tunnels beneath the city.

The cloaca maxima is still used for controlling stormwater. It is not the only Roman waterwork still in use. The Aqua Virgo brings water into Rome from a spring 10 miles (16 km) away to feed some of the city's famous fountains.

The Forum

The Forum grew into the business center of the city. Temples were built there, so it also became important for rituals. As the empire grew, rulers added to the Forum to celebrate their

∧ A caving expert explores a Roman aqueduct still in use beneath the city. About 90 percent of the ancient city remains buried and unexplored.

own glory. The first was Julius Caesar; the emperors Augustus, Vespasian, Nerva, and Trajan followed. The emperors also built other monuments, such as Trajan's column, which is carved with scenes of Rome's war against the Dacians of present-day Romania.

Prehistoric leader

Today the Forum is one of the most studied ancient sites in the world—but it still holds more secrets. In 2006 experts digging in Caesar's Forum, just yards away from a busy downtown street, turned up a new clue to the city's origins. On a cold winter morning, they lifted some heavy stone slabs and found themselves looking

∧ This photograph shows the center of Rome as it appears today. The large green space just beneath the center of the photograph is the Palatine Hill. Behind it are the ruins of the Colosseum. The long horizontal patch of green on the right is the Circus Maximus, which was used for chariot races.

∧ These scenes from Trajan's Column show Roman soldiers on campaign. Trajan brought the empire to its greatest size in A.D. 117.

into a 6-foot-deep (2 m) pit dug into the clay beneath.

Archaeologist Alessandro Delfino had already found two ancient tombs in the area. This pit was far bigger, and held a hut-shaped box that contained an urn filled with the ashes of a cremated body. The box also held bowls and jars buried along with the ashes. It was clear to Delfino and his team that the dead person must have been an important leader. But the

artifacts dated to about 1000 B.C.—250 years before the legendary founding of Rome, when farming peoples built the first settlements in the region.

More clues

The Forum has yielded so many discoveries that when American archaeologist Albert Ammerman was invited to work there in 1985, his first thought was that there was nothing left to discover. In fact, Ammerman was able to fill in details of the growth of the Forum. He used coring to test soil samples from different depths. A thin layer revealed that the Forum had been paved with gravel in the late seventh century B.C. By then, experts think, tribes in the area had united.

Master builders

The sequence of buildings in Rome show how the Romans developed their own building styles, based on Etruscan and Greek methods. The style combined columns, arches, and vaults. Long, thin bricks of baked clay were made to a standard size, which gave a characteristic appearance to the city. The Romans invented a type of concrete that they faced with stone or brick. It was lighter than stone. They also developed a barrel-shaped roof called a vault that could enclose large spaces. These technologies made the

Virtual Rome

The use of computer models to design new buildings is common in architecture, but archaeologists are now using the same techniques to reconstruct ancient buildings as a way to understand them better. The Cultural Virtual Reality Lab at the University of California, Los Angeles, has begun a project that will eventually lead to a virtual reconstruction of much of Ancient Rome. The reconstruction of the Colosseum, for example, has confirmed that it was a magnificent structure. But it has also shown that some of the passageways at the top of the structure were much smaller than had been thought. Some archaeologists, however, are not convinced about the value of virtual reality in showing people about the past. They say that the public cannot always understand what they see without some explanation.

creation of huge public buildings such as basilicas and baths possible. The Romans built the largest covered rooms in the ancient world.

Life in the circus

Public buildings were where people met, worshiped, and enjoyed themselves. The poet Juvenal moaned that his fellow citizens were only interested in "bread and circuses"—in having food to eat and entertainment.

The Circus Maximus was a popular destination. Romans went there to see high-speed chariot races held nearly every day around the oval track. The Colosseum staged displays by gladiators, who fought each other

V **This modern painting shows what the Colosseum might have looked like when it was flooded to stage sea battles.**

or wild animals. The discovery of pipes beneath the Colosseum may confirm accounts that it could be flooded to stage reenactments of sea battles.

The oval structure was so large that it could only have been built in Roman concrete. Stone would have been too heavy.

A masterpiece

Of all Rome's monuments, the best preserved is the only temple that honored all of the Romans' many gods:

∧ The Pantheon's dome is an awe-inspiring site for visitors. The ceiling still stands 1,800 years after it was built.

the Pantheon. Experts study the temple today to learn about Roman engineering. The concrete dome is light but strong: At the top, it is only 4 inches (10 cm) thick. The interior forms a sphere 141 feet (43 m) in diameter. The perfect dimensions reflect the skills of the Roman builders—skills that helped their creations stand for 2,000 years.

The Empire Spreads

Why did the Romans take over the Mediterranean?

Police chief Luigi Robusto could not believe his eyes. He was diving near the seabed off the port of Brindisi in southern Italy in the summer of 1992 when he noticed something sticking out of the sand: Greenish-colored human toes. For a terrible moment, Robusto thought he had discovered a body. When he touched the toes, however, he realized at once that they were metal. Robusto called in archaeologists. In the following weeks, they found a whole range of arms, heads, feet,

< Divers attach a rope to one of the pieces of bronze statue found on the seabed near Brindisi so that they can raise it to the surface.

ROMAN EMPIRE
ca 27 B.C. – 476 A.D.

| 200 | B.C. 0 A.D. | 200 | 400 | 600 |

and hands from bronze statues. They dated from the fourth century B.C. to the third century A.D. Sometime between the third and sixth centuries, archaeologists believe, the bronze was on board a boat heading for Brindisi. In a storm, the sailors threw the cargo over the side to lighten the load. The boat may even have sunk, although no physical remains of the vessel have been found

Archaeologists believe that the finds may show that the Romans were early recyclers. The bronzes may have been parts of old statues being taken to Brindisi to be melted down and reused, perhaps as weapons or armor. The statues may have been collected from eastern parts of the Mediterranean. By 44 B.C. the port at Brindisi linked Rome to territories throughout Greece, Turkey, the eastern Mediterranean, and Egypt.

A mystery circle

In 1995 archaeologist Angelo Pellegrino published a map of Ostia. The ancient port 15 miles (24 km) down the Tiber River from Rome had been widely excavated for

∧ The painting above shows divers rescuing the pieces of bronze from the bottom of the sea at Brindisi.

> The divers' haul included a range of disconnected body parts, leading to theories that the bronze was on its way to be melted down.

Roman coins

Roman coins had a standard size and value that made it easy to trade all over the empire. They were also a symbol of the power of Rome itself, which oversaw all minting of coins. Coins were made of gold, silver, and bronze. After 27 B.C. all new coins were marked with the image of the then emperor. That makes them a very useful tool for archaeologists trying to date their discoveries.

∧ This Roman coin (*front, right; reverse, above*) was discovered at Caesarea Maritima, an important eastern Mediterranean port in what is now Israel.

over 200 years. The new map showed an area north of the excavations, where an old branch of the Tiber had silted up. To the naked eye, the area was covered with empty fields—but Pellegrino's map showed the partial walls of a large, round structure.

Even apparently empty ground sometimes hides invisible treasures. To find those treasures, archaeologists need to get as high as possible. Photographs taken from the air show patterns of light and shade that cannot be seen from the ground. The patterns reveal buried walls, earthworks, or holes for fenceposts. Pellegrino spotted the building at Ostia in photographs taken from a balloon in 1911.

Later research seemed to confirm the building's shape—but what could it be? Norwegian archaeologist Jorgen

Christian Meyer suggested that it might be a circular tomb called a mausoleum. The building was huge, however: 215 feet (65 m) across. In Rome, such large mausoleums were reserved for the tombs of the emperors Augustus and Hadrian.

Whose tomb?

Might the building at Ostia be another imperial tomb? If so, whose? The answer was quite easy to find—if you followed the clues.

Clue one: When? Most building at Ostia dated from the first and second centuries A.D., so the mausoleum was likely built at about the same time. During that period Ostia was the most important port linking Rome with Spain, France, and North Africa. Excavations revealed warehouses

called *horrea* along the Tiber. They were used for storing goods.

Clue two: Why? In ancient times, the monument stood in a bend of the river where it was visible to everyone traveling to or from Ostia. It might have been intended to celebrate an emperor's link with the port.

Clue three: Scholars know the burial places of all first and second century emperors except two: Claudius and Vespasian. Of the two, one is an obvious choice. Claudius did more than any other emperor to make Ostia an important port. He dug out the harbor and had channels built from the Tiber to the sea. He built a lighthouse to guide sailors.

Empire and trade

Has Pellegrino located the tomb of Claudius? The jury's still out. More work is needed even to be sure that

∧ Caesarea Maritima did not have reliable water supplies of its own, so Herod built this aqueduct to bring water from a distance.

there is a mausoleum buried in the ground. But the facts fit what we know. Ostia was so vital to supplying Rome that the emperors took great interest in it.

One of the most important cargoes to pass through the port was food. Food shortages caused riots in Rome and even the overthrow of emperors. A stream of supplies was necessary to keep Rome's citizens happy. At the largest horrea in Ostia, raised floors protected the contents from damp and from vermin such as rats. Archaeologists believe that it may have been used to store grain. Rome's colonies in Sicily and North Africa supplied grain for the capital. The supply was so important that it was controlled by imperial officials.

A Roman port

Trade did not only supply Rome. It also helped hold the empire together. As areas were conquered, they were drawn into Rome's tax system and trade networks. The Romans made trade as easy as possible. Roman coins—denarii—turn up at sites all over the empire. They were the standard currency everywhere. There were no duties on imports and exports.

The remains of Caesarea Maritima, which is in present-day Israel, provide many clues about the importance of trade. The port was built by Herod the Great, the king who ruled the area for the Romans. Underwater excavations have found the two huge seawalls that protected the harbor. The walls were lined with warehouses. Written sources describe a lighthouse at the port whose flame never went out and giant bronze statues that stood on dangerous sandbars to warn sailors.

∧ Excavations take place near the Forum in Ostia, the port that served Rome; about 50,000 people lived in Ostia, which was also a naval base.

∨ This carving on a tomb shows the lighthouse that guided ships safely into the harbor at Ostia.

Underwater archaeology

Underwater archaeology is a fairly new way of learning about the past. It emerged in the 1950s and 1960s, when experts in ancient history began learning how to dive. They wanted to explore sunken ships, as well as coastal cities that have become submerged over time. Shipwrecks, for example, are one of the main sources of information about trade in the ancient world. Their cargoes are often intact, so experts can see what goods people wanted to buy.

Excavations on the seabed need the same amount of care as those on land. Divers record where they find everything before they lift it to the surface to be cleaned and examined. For depths that are too deep to reach by regular diving, archaeologists reach the seabed by using miniature submarines.

< Getting heavy objects to the surface requires the use of balloons that are inflated with air so that they rise through the water.

Shipwrecks at the station

In 1998 workers digging foundations for a railroad station in Pisa in western Italy found a well-preserved Roman ship. Construction had to stop and the area became an archaeological site. Further excavation revealed another sixteen ships dating from the first to sixth centuries A.D., and the remains of an ancient harbor. Pisa, standing on the Arno River near the coast, had been an Etruscan port before it became a Roman one.

So many ancient ships had not been found together before. The earth was very wet, which protected the

ships' timbers and stopped them from decaying. On one beam, excavators could even read the letters "O D A." Perhaps a bored sailor had passed the time by carving his initials. To protect the ships, the excavators encased them in a hard shell of resin and fiberglass.

Counting the cargo

The wet earth had also preserved what the ships were carrying. Some cargo was equipment for the sailors, such as ropes, fishing gear, anchors, lamps, winches, and fishing pots.

The ships also held traces of their other cargoes, which included wine

∧ Digging up the ships at Pisa took careful preservation work so that the old timbers did not decay when they came into contact with oxygen in the air.

and olive oil, as well as olives, cherries, and plums. One puzzle was reddish sand that could not have come from the Pisa region. Experts traced it to the Bay of Naples. Written records show that it was needed to make a sort of concrete that would set underwater.

The harbor at Pisa must have been a busy, noisy place. Ships unloaded supplies for the city or loaded marble or grain to carry north to Ostia and Rome. Similar scenes were repeated at ports throughout the empire. Archaeologists have found traces of a stunning variety of goods: corn, glassware, iron, lead, tin, leather, marble, olive oil, perfumes,

∧ These broken amphorae would have been used to transport liquids such as olive oil or wine.

purple dye, silk, silver, spices, timber, and wine, as well as slaves and livestock. The Romans conquered their empire by force—but in many ways they kept it together through trade.

CHAPTER 4

Far From the Capital

What was life like at the edges of the Empire?

About A.D. 100 the wife of a Roman commander on the northern edge of the empire received a short note from the wife of another commander. Claudia Severa greeted her friend Lepidina and requested: "On 11 September, sister, for the day of the celebration of my birthday, I give you a warm invitation to make sure that you come to us, to make the day more enjoyable for me by your arrival." The message, written in ink on a thin tablet of wood about the size

< This writing tablet from the Roman fort at Vindolanda in northern Britain contains Claudia Severa's birthday invitation to her friend.

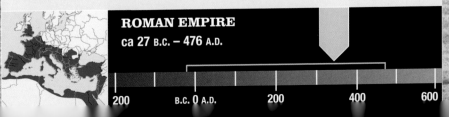

ROMAN EMPIRE
ca 27 B.C. – 476 A.D.

| 200 | B.C. 0 A.D. | 200 | 400 | 600 |

of a postcard was found in 1973 at Vindolanda, a fort on Hadrian's Wall. It was one of a collection of letters written in ink made of soot. Writing tablets like this were common in the Roman world; papyrus, paper made from reeds, was used only for important documents.

The Vindolanda tablets give a glimpse of life in the Roman army. They range from requests for leave of absence to requests for more supplies or for warmer clothes. Throughout the empire, Roman troops patrolled borders and garrisoned towns. They helped ensure peace and prosperity.

Empire of engineering

Wherever the Romans went, aqueducts, bathhouses, temples, and amphitheaters show how they

V Hadrian Wall—here crossing rocky crags in Northumbria—guarded Roman Britain from peoples who lived to the north.

Minimus: The mouse that made Latin cool

The Vindolanda letters inspired teachers in Britain to come up with a new book to teach Latin to children ages seven to ten. Minimus the mouse and Vibrissa the cat live with a real family who lived in Vindolanda in about A.D. 100: Flavius, the fort commander, his wife Lepidina, their three children, and the household slaves.

Latin and Roman culture are taught through lively illustrations, comic strips, and myths. The book also shows many of the artifacts and writing tablets from the Vindolanda excavations.

re-created many of the facilities of Rome itself. Even far from home, they had as many comforts as possible.

The Romans used natural springs to build large baths such as those at Bath in England. In cool countries they built homes with central heating.

> Charioteers like the one on this silver pot were stationed with the army throughout the empire.

Digs reveal columns that supported the floors, leaving a space beneath called the *hypocaust*. Pipes carried in hot air from furnaces to heat the floor.

Bath time

In 1998 a TV network invited leading experts on Roman baths to Bath. They faced a unique task: to build a working bath. Such reconstructions can be a useful way for archaeologists to test their theories about the past.

All Roman towns had public baths, and rich Romans had their own. They were not like tubs today. They cleaned people by using hot air to make them sweat, which brought dirt out of their skin. But how was the heat produced?

The experts chose a site near the Roman town of Sardis in Turkey to build a small bathhouse that might have belonged to a wealthy Roman. They mapped out three rooms. In the warm *tepidarium* bathers changed and scraped off dirt. They moved into a *caldarium,* which was so hot that they sweated heavily. They cooled down in the *frigidarium,* a room with a plunge

pool. Like the Romans, the team made sure that the caldarium faced the sun to get the most heat.

Local workers built the bathhouse using concrete made according to a Roman formula written down in the first century A.D. They mixed water with a powder called quicklime to form a paste to which they added stones and gravel. The roof was a vault, shaped like a half barrel. Keystones at the top stopped the sides from collapsing inward.

> The floor in this Roman building has been removed to show how the hypocaust worked. Hot air entered through small tunnels and circulated around the columns that supported the floor.

The Roman bath at Bath has been restored since the 18th century.

The spring that feeds the baths at Bath still runs through pipes built by the Romans.

Hot stuff

Next, heating experts moved in. They designed a furnace to heat water for a small pool in the caldarium. Hot air from the furnace would pass beneath the floor and up through hollows in the walls. The floors were covered in tiles based on Roman examples.

The experts lit the furnace. After a few minutes, smoke came out of the chimneys on top of the walls. The hot air was circulating. But how hot would it make the baths?

Next morning the team came back to try the first Roman bath for 1,500 years. Disaster! The concrete of the plunge pool had softened. Most of the water had run out through the walls. The experts had already found it difficult to make bricks and floor tiles that did not crack. Clearly they needed to learn more about Roman materials.

But what about the heating? The experts put on togas and entered the caldarium. The tiles were so hot that they had to wear sandals to walk on them. The system worked perfectly—even if there was no plunge pool to finish off the experience.

Roads to empire

Written sources

Some of the main sources for learning about life in the empire are written works. Julius Caesar, for example, wrote about his military campaigns in Gaul (modern France) and Britannia (modern Britain). He described his battles and was careful to show what a good general he was. But he also gave details about the peoples he defeated.

Such reports may be unreliable, but archaeologists can use them as a starting point. They can compare them with the physical evidence and with accounts from other writers. In that way, they can piece together a picture of life in the empire.

The Roman road network stretched 50,000 miles (80,000 km). Records show that the empire itself paid to build the most important roads; the army paid for roads that were used by the military. Local communities and landowners paid for other roads. The roads were generally planned to be straight so that journeys were as short as possible.

The building materials varied according to what was available in different places, but the method of construction was usually the same. From cross sections through roads, experts have learned that they were built on a raised embankment, called an agger, to help drain the surface. The top of the agger was covered with layers of fine material such as sand or gravel. On top, the road was paved with slabs of stone or with heavier pieces of gravel, flint, or another hard-wearing material.

∇ **A construction gang builds a road. Many roads were built by soldiers from the Roman army, partly to keep them busy during times of peace.**

The Buried Cities

CHAPTER 5

What was life like for the ordinary Romans?

In 1982, workers directed by Giuseppe Maggi began to excavate near the ancient seafront of Herculaneum, a Roman town on the Bay of Naples. On August 24 in A.D. 79, Herculaneum and the nearby town of Pompeii had been destroyed by the eruption of the volcano Vesuvius. Both towns had been buried beneath layers of ash and lava and forgotten until they were accidentally found at the end of the 16th century. Both sites have been well investigated by archaeologists. At Pompeii, they

< Bone analysis has shown that this skeleton from Herculaneum belonged to a 45-year-old woman. She still wears two gold rings on the fingers of her left hand.

ROMAN EMPIRE
ca 27 B.C. – 476 A.D.

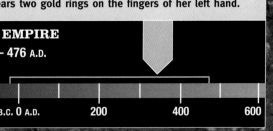

| 200 | | B.C. 0 A.D. | | 200 | | 400 | | 600 |

∧ Expert Vittorio De Girolamo clears earth from the skeleton of a soldier at Herculaneum, identified by the sword that lies at his side.

> The ash and lava that covered Pompeii and Herculaneum preserved many buried paintings and sculptures, like this bust of a young woman.

found the remains of citizens who had suffocated as they tried to escape. At Herculaneum, experts believed, most people had gotten out alive.

Skeleton keys

Maggi discovered a different story. In a boathouse near the old seafront he found a cluster of skeletons: seven adults, four children, and a baby. He reckoned they were a household trying to flee. Next door were skeletons charred by a flow of fiery rock and debris that spilled out of the volcano. Another skeleton on the beach was that of a soldier who may have been trying to control the crowd. His sword lay by his side. There was also a boat: Perhaps someone had been trying to put to sea to escape.

Bad bones

The new finds at Herculaneum drew many experts, including some who were sponsored by the National Geographic Society. The Romans usually cremated their dead, so few skeletons had survived. Now there were many to study.

Analysis of bones can reveal a lot about what people ate or whether they suffered from any diseases. At Herculaneum, experts found, people had suffered from lead poisoning. They believe that this may have been the result of drinking cheap wine, which was stored in lead containers.

Time capsules

The disaster that destroyed Pompeii and Herculaneum has been a blessing for archaeologists. The two cities are like time capsules. They allow experts to fill in the details that may not have survived at many other Roman sites. They show exactly what everyday life was like for the Romans.

∨ In this painting, a fast-moving wave of superhot volcanic debris—called the pyroclastic flow— overwhelms victims on the seafront at Herculaneum.

What a load of rubbish

A remarkable record of ordinary life lies on the edge of Rome: a mountain of trash about 135 feet (45 m) high. Monte Testaccio is a pile of millions of broken amphorae thrown away by between the first and third centuries. The jugs were mass-produced and cheap, so they were often thrown away after they had been used rather than being cleaned out. The jugs were used to transport olive oil to Rome from areas around the Mediterranean, mainly from what is now Andalucia in Spain. Many of the amphorae are marked with the seals of their makers or with notes recording their contents. The details make Monte Testaccio a record not just of Roman trade but also of the inhabitants' eating habits.

When the jugs were thrown away, the broken pieces were scattered with powdered lime to stop any old oil from rotting. The lime stuck the pottery together and made the pile stable. The "mountain" became a popular landmark for Romans. Over the centuries cellars, cafés, and even nightclubs have been dug into its base.

‹ Rome's trendy nightclub Fake is built right into the hill of trash at Monte Testaccio, where dancers are surrounded by pieces of broken pottery.

Pompeii and Herculaneum were lively seaside towns; each had a population of about 10,000 citizens. After the eruption of Vesuvius the area was a desert of ash. The sites were abandoned. Soil settled over the towns and they disappeared from sight for 1,700 years.

Remains of Pompeii were spotted in 1594, and in 1710 pieces of fine marble from Herculaneum were discovered. Later, the king of Naples

had the sites excavated in the hopes of finding ancient treasure. In Pompeii it was relatively easy to dig through the ash, but in Herculaneum the lava had turned to hard rock. The treasure seekers did not take much care. They

∧ Wealthy Roman homes were arranged around a courtyard that helped keep them cool and private. In the large room at the top of the painting is a dining room with couches: The Romans liked to eat lying down. In the kitchen at left, slaves are preparing food for a meal.

∧ Plaster casts like this reveal the last moments of the victims at Pompeii. This man had huddled desperately into a corner and tried to cover his mouth for protection from the hot ash raining down on the town.

Getting scientific

The first scientific excavations began in 1860 under the archaeologist Giuseppe Fiorelli. He introduced a new system of uncovering houses from the top down, which helped preserve anything that was discovered. He also developed a system to identify hollows found in the solidified ash. The spaces had been made by objects that had since rotted away—including the bodies of people or animals. Fiorelli drilled a small hole to fill the hollow with liquid plaster. When the plaster hardened, the surrounding ash could be removed to reveal an image of the original. The method is still used today using fiberglass instead of plaster; fiberglass is transparent and can reveal bones and jewelry that might have been trapped inside the hollows. In areas that were made airtight by the mud, mainly in Herculaneum, even perishable objects such as papyrus scrolls survived.

Treasure troves of the past

The buried towns still hold more secrets. Only three-fifths of Pompeii has been uncovered, and even less of Herculaneum. But they have already provided a detailed picture of Roman life. Pompeii and Herculaneum were both prosperous towns in a fertile region that was popular with wealthy Romans. Many people kept vacation

were only looking for valuable objects, and they caused much damage to the buildings. They removed objects without recording them, and stripped paintings and mosaics from the walls and floors. The discoveries began a fashion among Europe's rulers and wealthy citizens to collect objects from Ancient Rome.

homes there. They were decorated with painted murals, fine statues, and mosaics. In Pompeii, well-paved streets had high sidewalks and stepping stones to keep pedestrians out of the mud. Around the forum were temples, a market, and a basilica. For relaxation there were several baths, an amphitheater for watching gladiators or chariot races, and two theaters to watch plays.

New buildings are still being uncovered. They are found just as they were left, even with pots on the stove—sometimes still holding the remains of a meal. But many experts believe that the rest of the town should be left for future generations to uncover. Rather than excavating further, they want to concentrate on conserving the many treasures that have already been revealed.

⋀ This floor mosaic from Pompeii warns visitors to *"Cave canem"*—"Beware of the dog."

⋁ National Geographic photographer James L. Stanfield gets an unusual shot—from inside a Roman toilet. The Romans went to the bathroom together in rooms with special benches around the walls.

Meet an Archaeologist

Alan Kaiser of the University of Evansville, Indiana, has excavated ruins throughout the Roman world. He uses new technology to map how the Romans used space in their cities for different activities.

What made you want to be an archaelogist?
I love mysteries and puzzles and the past is filled with them. I knew I would be excited if I dug something up and had absolutely no idea what it was or how it was used. It is great fun to try to find answers to these questions.

When did you get interested in ancient Rome?
I first studied the Romans in college and then took a summer trip to Italy. I walked on top of aqueducts, I stood in the Colosseum in Rome, I looked at plaster casts of bodies from Pompeii, and was in awe.

What's the best part of your job?
Travel. I have eaten lunch at the base of Mt. Vesuvius, watched the moon set over the Straits of Actium where Augustus defeated Antony and Cleopatra, and sneaked past a herd of bulls while searching for Roman sites in Spain. Doing what I love has brought me to some very interesting places—and it has introduced me to new people. I have made friends in Italy, Spain, England, Greece, and other places, and even though language and culture divide us, our passion for the past creates a bond of friendship.

What's the worst part of your job?

Raising money for field work. It costs a great deal to run an excavation or do any type of archaeological field work so I have to apply for grants. It is hard to ask people for money.

What are the most important qualities for an archaeologist?
1) patience; you must work slowly so as not to damage artifacts;
2) ability to study and fit into modern foreign cultures;
3) patience; something is always going to go wrong;
4) hard work and good grades so you can get into college;
5) patience—becoming an archaeologist takes many years.

◘ Is there much still left to learn about the ancient Romans?

◙ Many, many unanswered questions remain about the Romans. Why did the Roman Empire fall? How old was the average Roman child when he or she started working?

◘ What was the most exciting discovery you've ever made?

◙ I found a piece of pottery with two finger impressions in it. I put my fingers where the potter had and I understood at once that he had been trying to even out one side of the pot. For a split second time and space disappeared and I had the same thought as one ancient person.

◘ Do you have any advice for young children who want to become archaeologists?

◙ 1) Do well in school.
2) Ask your parents to bring you to visit museums and archaeological sites.
3) Study history to learn what cultures interest you.
4) Learn a foreign language.

◘ Do you need to learn Latin to study the Romans?

◙ Yes. You cannot truly understand any culture without learning its language. But learning Latin is fun. When you read Caesar's account of the Gallic wars in the original Latin, you feel like you are standing beside him,

∧ Alan Kaiser keys information into a computer in his "lab" at the Roman site of Ampurias in Spain. He feeds data into a program that creates digital maps of Roman cities.

sword drawn, ready to fight the Gauls.

◘ Why did the Roman Empire fall?

◙ There are many theories, and I don't know which is correct. Perhaps someone from the next generation of archaeologists will be able to figure out a final answer to that question: But I don't think that it will be simple.

◘ Can movies like *Ben Hur* or *Gladiator* tell us much about ancient Rome?

◙ Books and movies about ancient Rome tell us more about ourselves than the Romans. In *Ben Hur*, *Gladiator*, and *Spartacus* a

slave challenges the empire and becomes a hero. These movies show us we are fascinated by the ordinary person who overcomes great odds.

◘ What have you learned from mapping different Roman cities?

◙ While drawing maps of Roman cities and analyzing them using a Geographic Information Systems computer program, I discovered that certain streets were closed to cart traffic or had obstacles that made it very difficult for carts to get around. Now I'm trying to figure out why; what made those streets so special?

The Fall of Rome

What happened to ancient Rome?

In the centuries around A.D. 1000 large areas of Rome lay abandoned. The city that had once been home to some two million people now had a population of only about 20,000. Vegetation covered disused temples and palaces. A visitor found cows grazing in the ancient Forum. What was left of the Roman Empire was ruled from a new capital, Constantinople in what is now Turkey. The empire had been split into two in the fourth century. The western part had been defeated in the fifth century.

Rome had not disappeared, however. There were signs everywhere of its legacy, from its physical

< Traffic speeds past the Colosseum in the heart of Rome at night. Signs of the ancient culture are still visible not just in Rome but throughout the empire.

remains to Latin words that were still used in European languages.

A mysterious end

What had happened to Rome? Scholars have been thinking about that mystery for centuries. There is no single answer, but clues may lie in farmland in northwest Germany. In 1987 British army captain Tony Clunn took a posting at the nearby city of Osnabrück. Clunn was an amateur archaeologist who was eager to look around. He believed the area may have been the site of the Battle of Teutoberg, fought in A.D. 9 between Roman troops and Germanic warriors. The Germans had defeated three legions—and signaled the beginning of the end for the empire. The director of the Osnabrück museum, Wolfgang Schlüter, suggested that Clunn explore near a hill named Kalkriese, where Roman coins had been found.

Coins are clues

Clunn studied old maps and focused on a space between Kalkriese and what was once a bog. Anyone in the area, he reasoned, would have passed through the gap. When Clunn used his metal detector,

< Constantine made Constantinople the eastern capital in A.D. 330. This 8-foot 6-inch (2.5 m) head of the first Christian emperor of Rome was part of a statue that stood 40 feet (12 m) tall.

it did not take long before the machine's alarm sounded. Clunn dug only a few inches before he hit paydirt: a denarius, black with age. It bore the face of an emperor he recognized, Augustus. Within minutes he found another coin, and then a third. Within two days, he had found 89 coins. Who had lost them?

Further finds made the picture clearer. Coins, nails from sandals, shards of metal, and human bones were scattered over a fan-shaped area. Other objects helped to identify their owners: Sheaths for swords and balls of metal thrown in sling shots must have belonged to soldiers. There was also a face mask that once protected a standard-bearer. The standard-bearer

Metal mayhem

Many archaeologists are wary of people with metal detectors. They worry that amateurs are more interested in treasure than in finding out about the past. Treasure hunters may not keep accurate records of where they find objects—which can be as revealing as what is found. Metal detectors do not find objects made of wood, stone, or bone. Untrained enthusiasts may overlook them or, even worse, destroy them by digging carelessly. Amateurs may also get a bad name by not seeking permission from landowners before they start digging.

In the right hands, however, metal detectors can be very useful tools. As Tony Clunn showed at Kalkriese, the alarm signal in a treasure hunter's headphones might be the start of a really important find.

∧ Recovered from the battlefield at Kalkriese, this holder once fastened a Roman officer's scabbard to his belt.

< Pieces of a horse harness were among more than 5,000 objects found over a large area at Kalkriese.

55

carried his unit's symbol on a long pole. He was a vital rallying point on the battlefield. To let a standard be captured by the enemy was a great disgrace for a Roman soldier.

Clunn believed the objects were dropped by Roman troops running away from the point of the fan shape. What were they fleeing? Easy: The warriors of Arminius, a Germanic leader who had once served in a Roman legion but now led his army against the empire. Clunn had found the lost battlefield of Teutoberg.

The fall of Rome

Defeat at Teutoberg was not the end of Rome. In fact, the empire grew for another century. But the defeat was a

Lasting Latin

One of the great legacies of the Roman Empire was its language. Latin was used everywhere. Classical Latin was more formal and was used for poetry. Vulgar Latin was for everyday use. As the Empire broke up in the fifth century, Vulgar Latin split into dialects that became languages such as Italian, French, and Spanish. Classical Latin was kept alive only by the Roman Catholic Church. In the eastern empire and in Spain, however, scholars studied Latin works. In the Renaissance that knowledge passed back to Europe, as educated people became interested in classical culture. Latin became the universal language of learning, a position it retained until the 19th century.

sign of trouble ahead. It was the first evidence that the imperial army could be beaten. By the end of the second century A.D. the empire was so large that it had become difficult to protect its borders. Over the next 150 years its neighbors launched raids into the empire. Local chieftains took power. The economy broke up, which undermined the authority of the emperors in Rome.

In 395 A.D. the Roman Empire was divided into east and west. In the west, the last emperor was

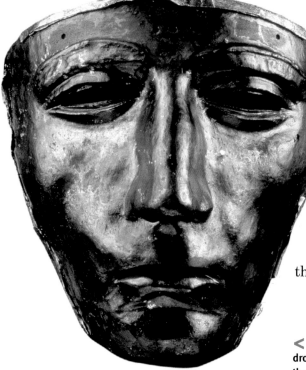

◁ This mask from Kalkriese was probably dropped by a standard-bearer trying to flee the Germanic warriors.

defeated in A.D. 476 by a Germanic people called Visigoths. The eastern Roman Empire survived until 1453, when it fell to the Ottoman Turks.

After Rome

The collapse of the empire had a huge impact on Europe. Trade declined as pirates and robbers made travel dangerous. Authorities could no longer maintain roads. Cities were deserted. The ability to read largely vanished across Europe: Even kings could rarely read.

Historians used to call the period after the fall of Rome the "Dark Ages." In fact art and learning continued, in Europe's monasteries and in the empire in the east, now called the Byzantine Empire. But the idea that the civilization had simply ended was powerful. It appealed to the Italians of the 13th and 14th centuries. By then, trade had revived and Italy's cities were growing rich. Wealth spurred a revival of interest in Ancient Rome. Scholars saw the classical period of Greece and Rome as the source of European civilization. Artists and sculptors copied Roman examples. Architects built in Roman styles. The movement was later named the Renaissance or "rebirth." It was a return to classical tradition—and to the days of Rome's glory.

▽ A young tourist clowns with actors dressed as Roman soldiers during a visit to the Colosseum.

The Years Ahead

One of the main problems facing archaeologists who study Ancient Rome is that there is too much material to study. The empire covered such a large area for such a long time that it is impossible to study everything.

Sometimes it is impossible even to save everything. In 1998 in the small town of Ecija in Spain, for example, archaeologists discovered ancient remains during the construction of a parking lot. They identified the ruins as the forum of a Roman city named Colonia Augusta Firma Astigi. The experts were thrilled: The city was said to be one of the greatest of Roman Spain. But their delight soon turned to dismay. The town council ruled in 2006 that the parking lot needed to be built anyway. The 2,000-year-old city was covered with concrete—and is now lost once more. Such incidents are sometimes inevitable: Some people believe that there are so many Roman remains that we cannot preserve them all. Experts should concentrate only on the most important.

Another debate that may impact the future of Roman archaeology is about the ownership of artifacts. Italian authorities estimate that one historical artifact, including Roman objects, is being stolen every hour by looters. There are so many priceless artifacts that sometimes the theft is not even noticed. Some pieces find their way into museums around the world. People who worked for museums were put on trial for buying stolen antiquities. Some museums began to negotiate the return of objects that the Italians say were stolen. Other experts argue that musuems should be allowed to keep artifacts that they bought if there was no reason to believe that they were stolen.

◁ A worker inspects a bronze Roman vase in a police warehouse in Rome used to store stolen works of art that have been recovered.

Glossary

amphitheater – an oval or circular building with rows of seats, used for staging sports or other events

aqueduct – a channel or pipe that carries water from one place to another

artifact – any object changed by human activity

assassinate – to murder someone for a political reason

basilica – a rectangular building with a semicircular end used as a court of justice and a place for public meetings; the same name was also used for an early Christian church.

ceramics – objects made from clay and fired at high temperatures

circa – about; used to indicate a date that is approximate, and abbreviated as ca

circus – a large arena surrounded by rows of seats and used for sports such as chariot racing or other events

colosseum – a large ampitheater for games and other public events. The most famous example was built in Rome.

consul – an official elected to govern the Roman republic for a year

coring – a way of studying layers in the ground by drilling a small but deep hole to extract samples of soil

dictator – a leader who has complete control over a country and does not have to be elected or re-elected to office regularly

economy – the system by which a country creates wealth through making and trading products

empire – a large area in which different territories or peoples are ruled by an emperor

excavation – an archaeological dig

forum – a marketplace or public area in a Roman city that was the center for business and civic events

gladiator – a person who took part in fights staged for a public audience

legend – a fantastic story that may have some basis in real events

legion – a unit of the Roman army with between 3,000 and 6,000 foot soldiers, named legionnaires, and cavalry

mosaic – a picture or design made from small pieces of stone or glass

peninsula – land that is nearly surrounded by water

relief – a sculpture that is raised from a flat surface

Renaissance – a word meaning "rebirth," used to describe the renewed interest in the classical world in the 1400s and 1500s in Europe

republic – a type of government in which a state is governed by a group of citizens

rituals – repeated practices that relate to specific, often religious, ceremonies

scabbard – a case for a sword

stratigraphy – the study of different layers, or strata, of remains in the ground

survey – a careful collection of data about an area or subject

tablet – a thin, flat slab for writing on

tax – money paid to the government and used to run the country

theory – in science, the explanation that best fits the available evidence

vault – a barrel-shaped roof or underground chamber

Bibliography

Books

Corbishley, Mike. *Ancient Rome* (Cultural Atlas for Young People). New York: Chelsea House Publishers, 2007.

Pompeii: The Vanished City (Lost Civilizations series). Alexandria, VA: Time-Life Books, 1992.

Rome: Echoes of Imperial Glory (Lost Civilizations series). Alexandria, VA: Time-Life Books, 1994.

Articles

Bennett, Paul. "In Rome's Basement" NATIONAL GEOGRAPHIC (July 2006): 88–103.

Gore, Rick. "The Dead Do Tell Tales at Vesuvius." NATIONAL GEOGRAPHIC (May 1984): 557–613.

Reid, T. R. "The Power and the Glory of the Roman Empire." NATIONAL GEOGRAPHIC (July 1997): 2–41.

Reid, T. R. "The World According to Rome." NATIONAL GEOGRAPHIC. (August 1997): 54–83.

Further Reading

Ancient Rome (DK Eyewitness Books). New York: DK Publishing, 2004.

Corbishley, Mike. *The British Museum Illustrated Encyclopaedia of Ancient Rome*. London: British Museum Press, 2003.

Lewis, Jon E. (ed.). *The Mammoth Book of Eyewitness Ancient Rome: The History of the Rise and Fall of the Roman Empire in the Words of Those Who Were There*. New York: Carroll and Graf, 2003.

On the Web

BBC Romans homepage
http://www.bbc.co.uk/schools/romans/

History for Kids Roman page
www.historyforkids.org/learn/romans/

PBS Roman Empire site
http://www.pbs.org/empires/romans//

Roman Empire.net
http://www.roman-empire.net/children/index.html

TeacherNet Roman links
http://members.aol.com/TeacherNet/AncientRome.html

ndex

Boldface indicates illustrations.

About the Author

ZILAH DECKKER trained as an architectural historian and earned a PhD from the University of East Anglia before becoming a writer. She has contributed to many publications, including academic encyclopedias on a wide range of subjects, the *Dictionary of Art* (1996), and the *Encyclopedia of Architectural Technology* (2002), and is the author of *Brazil Built: The Architecture of the Modern Movement in Brazil* (2001).

About the Consultant

ROBERT LINDLEY VANN studied classical archaeology before becoming a professor of architecture at the University of Maryland. He has excavated classical sites in Italy, Turkey, Tunisia, Israel, and Jordan. He is director of a project at Pompeii that focuses on food and drink and the role they played in Roman life.

> A second-century-A.D. pottery vase made in central Gaul. The clay was thrown in a mold mounted on a potter's wheel. The mold pressed a design onto the vessel.

One of the world's largest nonprofit scientific and educational organizations, the National Geographic Society was founded in 1888 "for the increase and diffusion of geographic knowledge." Fulfilling this mission, the Society educates and inspires millions every day through its magazines, books, television programs, videos, maps and atlases, research grants, the National Geographic Bee, teacher workshops, and innovative classroom materials. The Society is supported through membership dues, charitable gifts, and income from the sale of its educational products. This support is vital to National Geographic's mission to increase global understanding and promote conservation of our planet through exploration, research, and education.

For more information, please call 1-800-NGS-LINE (647-5463) or write to the following address:

National Geographic Society
1145 17th Street N.W.
Washington, D.C. 20036-4688
U.S.A.

Visit the Society's Web site:
www.nationalgeographic.com

Library of Congress Cataloging-in-Publication Data available upon request
Hardcover ISBN: 978-1-4263-0128-5
Library Edition ISBN: 978-1-4263-0129-2

Printed in Mexico

Series design by Jim Hiscott
The body text is set in Century Schoolbook
The display text is set in Helvetica Neue, Clarendon

National Geographic Society

John M. Fahey, Jr., *President and Chief Executive Officer;* Gilbert M. Grosvenor, *Chairman of the Board;* Nina D. Hoffman, *Executive Vice President, President of Book Publishing Group*

Staff for This Book

Nancy Laties Feresten, *Vice President, Editor-in-Chief of Children's Books*
Virginia Ann Koeth, *Project Editor*
Bea Jackson, *Director of Design and Illustration*
David M. Seager, *Art Director*
Lori Epstein, National Geographic Image Sales, *Illustrations Editors*
Jean Cantu, *Illustrations Specialist*
Priyanka Lamichhane, *Assistant Editor*
R. Gary Colbert, *Production Director*

Lewis R. Bassford, *Production Manager*
Maryclare Tracy, Nicole Elliott, *Manufacturing Managers*
Maps, *Mapping Specialists, Ltd.*

For the Brown Reference Group, plc
Tim Cooke, *Editor*
Alan Gooch, *Book Designer*
Encompass Graphics, *Cartographers*

Photo Credits
Front: Guenter Rossenbach/Zefa/Corbis
Back: Erich Lessing/Art Resource NY
Spine: Tiberius Dinu/Shutterstock
Icon: David McKee/Shutterstock

NGIC = National Geographic Image Collection
1, © Eric Lessing/AKG; 2–3, © O. Louis Mazzatenta/NGIC; 4, © O. Louis Mazzatenta/NGIC; 6, © Tiberius Dinu/Shutterstock; 10, © AKG; 11t , © Museum Kalkriese/AKG; 11b, © Erich Lessing/AKG; 12–13, © Stephen Alvarez/NGIC; 14, © James L. Stanfield/NGIC 15, © James L. Stanfield/NGIC; 16, © Thomas J. Abercrombie/NGIC; 17, © Javaman/Shutterstock; 18, © James L. Stanfield/ NGIC; 19, © James L. Stanfield /NGIC; 20–21, © Reuters/Corbis; 22, © James L. Stanfield/NGIC; 23, © Stephen Alvarez/NGIC; 24t, © Stephen Alvarez/NGIC; 24b, © O. Loius Mazzatenta/NGIC; 25, © James L. Stanfield/NGIC; 26, © HM Herget/NGIC; 27, © Everett Johnson/Folio Inc; 28–29, © O. Louis Mazzantenta/ NGIC; 30t, © Gregory Harlin/NGIC; 30b, © O. Louis Mazzatenta/NGIC; 31l, © Bill Curtsinger/NGIC; 31r, © Bill Curtsinger/NGIC; 32, © Ira Block/NGIC; 33t, © James L. Stanfield/NGIC; 33b, © James L. Stanfield/ NGIC; 34, © Bill Curtsinger/NGIC; 35t, © Muzzi Fabio/ Corbis; 35b, © Muzzi Fabio/Corbis; 36–37, © Vindolanda Trust; 38, © Terry Walsh/Shutterstock; 39t, © Robert Sheridan/Ancient Art and Architecture Collection Ltd; 39b, © Topham; 40t, © M. Birkitt/Topham; 40b, © Adam Woolfitt/Corbis; 41, © Christopher Klein/NGIC; 42–43, © Jonathan Blair/NGIC; 44t, © Jonathan Blair/NGIC; 44b, © O. Louis Mazzatenta/ NGIC; 45, © William H. Bond/NGIC; 46, © Stephen Alvarez/NGIC; 46–47, © Harry Bliss/NGIC; 48, © Bettmann/ Corbis; 49t, © Alinari/Topham; 49b, © Ken Kobersteen/ NGIC; 50, © Alan Kaiser, Evansville University, Indiana; 51, © Alan Kaiser, Evansville University, Indiana; 52–53, © Joel Sartore/NGIC; 54, © Merle Severy/NGIC; 55t, © Museum Kalkriese/AKG; 55b, © Museum Kalkriese/ AKG; 56, © Museum Kalkriese/AKG; 57, © James L. Stanfield/NGIC; 58, © O. Louis Mazzatenta/NGIC; 63, © British Museum/HIP/Topham

Front cover: Detail of the head of Constantine from a huge statue that once stood in Rome.
Page 1 and back cover: A limestone carving of a lion from a 1st-century-A.D. Roman grave in Tunisia.
Pages 2–3: A horse-drawn cart passes broken statues on the Appian Way, a Roman road outside Rome.

NATIONAL GEOGRAPHIC
EOGRAPHIC INVESTIGAG
NVESTIGATES NATIONAL
ES NATIONAL GEOGRAPH
L GEOGRAPHIC INVESTIG
C INVESTIGATES NATIO
ATES NATIONAL GEOGRA
NAL GEOGRAPHIC INVES
PHIC INVESTIGATES NAT
GATES NATIONAL GEOG
ONAL GEOGRAPHIC INVE
RAPHIC INVESTIGATES N
STIGATES NATIONAL GEO
ATIONAL GEOGRAPHIC IN
OGRAPHIC INVESTIGATE
NVESTIGATES NATIONAL
S NATIONAL GEOGRAPHI